EVALUATING PLAYS ON FILM AND VIDEO

Anne Marie Welsh
University of California, San Diego

Martin Morawski
University of California, Irvine

PEARSON
Longman

New York Boston San Francisco
London Toronto Sydney Tokyo Singapore Madrid
Mexico City Munich Paris Cape Town Hong Kong Montreal

Acquisitions Editor: Erika Berg
Senior Supplements Editor: Donna Campion
Cover Design: Teresa Ward
Project Manager: Kim Rossi

Evaluating Plays on Film and Video, by Anne Marie Welsh and Martin Morawski

ISBN: 0-321-18794-6

1 2 3 4 5 6 7 8 9 10–DPC–06 05 04 03

EVALUATING PLAYS ON FILM AND VIDEO
TABLE OF CONTENTS

iv

EVALUATING PLAYS ON FILM AND VIDEO

INTRODUCTION

Why write about plays on film?

During the past decade, scores of stage directors have transformed plays into movies. From the complete works of Samuel Beckett (now available on DVD) to writer-filmmaker Neil LaBute's compelling *In the Company of Men* and *The Shape of Things*, to Kenneth Branagh's *Much Ado About Nothing*, Julie Taymor's *Titus* and other Shakespeare-based movies, these cinematic versions of plays come in a time-honored tradition that is as old as filmmaking itself.

Many of the first silent films were inspired by Shakespeare's action-packed and talk-filled plays. With the advent of sound recording, American playwrights who wrote in the realist tradition provided ready-made scripts for filmmakers and soon came to see their works "opened up" for the silver screen. Thornton Wilder's popular *Our Town* (1939) became a feature film the next year, although it changed to suit the tastes of the general American public. The first draft of Tennessee William's *The Glass Menagerie* was actually a screenplay for MGM titled *The Gentleman Caller.* Soon, the nation's playwrights came almost to expect that their work would eventually be filmed.

Most of Williams' plays, for instance, became feature films, often with the same actors who had made the plays successful on Broadway. Marlon Brando and Vivien Leigh played Stanley Kowalski and Blanche Du Bois in stage and screen versions of *A Streetcar Named Desire*, both directed by Elia Kazan. Eugene O'Neill's work, as well as Arthur Miller's, has often been filmed, with varying degrees of success. Some of the plays have been adapted for the screen so frequently that comparing the films is both possible and useful.

During the 1950s, when television was still a new medium, live television productions of plays – including such important modern landmarks as Henrik Ibsen's *A Doll's House* with Julie Harris and Christopher Plummer – were broadcast weekly on dramatic presentations such as "Playhouse 90" and "Omnibus." Luminaries such as Orson Welles, the actor, stage director, and creator of the great film *Citizen Kane,* often directed these TV presentations. Videos of many of these early Golden Age of Television productions are now available. Although live television dramas are a thing of the past, cable networks are again airing made-for-television films adapted from plays; HBO, public television's WNET, and Showtime are three of the most active producers in this field.

Whether the film director is a film specialist or goes back and forth between the worlds of stage and screen, he or she may take a variety of approaches to staging dramas and comedies for the camera, rather than for a live audience in a theater. When you watch one of these films with awareness, then analyze it for the director's strategy, the quality of the acting, the film's mood, the atmosphere, and the emotional impact, you will learn a great deal about both the source play and the artist who directed it for the screen. You will also, of course, learn something about yourself. Playwrights and film directors create work for audiences – not just for themselves or a small group of their friends. Their work is meant to be seen and heard. The very personal process of responding to a play on film, then writing your response in a coherent review or longer essay, actually completes the circle of communication initiated by the playwright and visualized by the director.

Writing about plays on film, however, can be a more complex process than analyzing a play on the page or reviewing one on the stage. So be ready to spend several hours **preparing** to write about the film by first studying the play as it was written and comparing your impressions of that basic text (a script, actually) with your experience of the film. Careful comparison and questioning will be the keys to understanding and writing well about any play on film or video.

I. PREPARING

Traditionally, theater has been mostly a verbal medium. A playwright's poetic words may create detailed imagery in a reader's mind, but most scripts take on their strongest visual component when they are fully realized – with sets, costumes, lights, actors and sound – on a stage. Theater is also live, and therefore dangerous. Actors can make mistakes, and scenery can fall. Film, by contrast, is mostly a visual medium with the written screenplay and the characters' dialogue a much smaller element of the production. With characteristically dry humor, the great director of dark thrillers, Alfred Hitchcock, once remarked cavalierly about verbal language. He said he was ready to shoot the scene once the screenplay was complete "and the dialogue added." In film, also, mistakes can be edited out. The final print, then, is a fixed product. From these basic contrasts flow a series of other differences between stage and screen presentation. By thinking about and understanding these differences, you can begin to form a useful new set of expectations about plays on film. A film need not be a word-for-word, scene-for-scene, completely faithful visualization of the play for it to be valid. Many films become separate works of art precisely because they are not literally faithful to the source play. Instead, they capture the essence of a playwright's vision in a new medium.

Study this list of basic differences and see if you can think of specific examples – perhaps a stage production of *Romeo and Juliet* which you saw in high school compared to Baz Luhrmann's

996 punk-styled film starring Leonardo DiCaprio and Claire Danes; or a live production of Arthur Miller's *Death of a Salesman* and the often-televised video version with Dustin Hoffman. Several contrasts in the following chart were outlined in *As You Like It: Audio-Visual Shakespeare*, edited by C. Grant and *What is Cinema?* by Andre Bazin. Other differences are from observation. Perhaps you can think of more.

Key differences between stage and screen productions

Verbal Medium/Live Performance	Visual Medium/ Fixed Film or Video
Happens now; made fresh each time the play is performed	Fixed in its time of making; a finished product
Performers present; limited in number	Performers absent (virtual image); unlimited number
Audience integral and acknowledged as a group or community	Audience is separate; responding individually
Audience's physical relationship to stage and actors is fixed	Audience viewpoint shifted by director
Audience chooses where to look and focus	Director determines audience focus
Action confined to stage space; language and imagination conjure other places in the mind	Action occurs in many locales, settings and set decoration physically realized rather than imagined
Actors often enter and leave	Actors can be "discovered" in the space and seen traveling to other spaces
Characters consistent in size and visible from head to toe	Characters change size; often only portions of the body seen: close-up
Character movement limited	Movement virtually unlimited
Script allows players to externalize emotion	Screenplay often internalizes feeling
Special effects limited and costly	Special effects relatively easy, frequent
Complete scene is basic structural unit	Each shot is the unit of construction
Illusion of reality based on evocative use of language; stage visible.	Illusion of reality created by visual images; no visible stage
Viewer feels tension between himself and the actors	Viewer more easily identifies with actor, gives self over to the illusion

Step 1: Describing the play's elements

Knowing the literary classification of the play and understanding its action, characters and style will prepare you to assess the film. It is best to begin with genre.

Genre:

There are six basic types of play. The ancient Greek philosopher Aristotle wrote one of the earliest, and still one of the most useful, descriptions of drama in his *Poetics*. There, he classified the first two genres as tragedy and comedy. The basic outcome of the action determines whether a play is a strict tragedy, which ends with the hero's downfall, or comedy, which generally ends happily for the main characters. Since that ancient era, four other forms have emerged: history and mixed forms, melodrama, tragicomedy, and musical theatre.

Review the six basic types of play:

- Tragedy
- Comedy
- History
- Melodrama
- Tragicomedy
- Musical Theatre

Comedy can be further divided into such sub-genres as farce, satire, and the comedy of manners. Today many critics feel that the age of tragedy has passed; psychology and democracy have replaced the sense of mystery and greatness of character that are necessary, at least according to Aristotle, for an action to have tragic dimension. The mixed mode of tragicomedy, these scholars argue, best reflects the actual complexity and diminishment of modern life. Tragicomedy is the prevalent genre today.

Plot and action:

Aristotle wrote that plot is the "soul" of drama, more important even than character. But clearly the Greek plays that this first literary critic studied were not always action-filled epics. In fact, most of the events in classic tragedy took place off-stage, with the onstage characters, and the chorus, reacting to reports of events – for instance, Phedre deciding to kill herself for shame when it's reported that her husband, whom she has betrayed, is still alive. External events in a melodrama (Victor Hugo's *Hernani* for instance, or in Ibsen's *A Doll's House* which still bears traces of melodrama in its subplot) may be an important dramatic element. More often, however, especially in modern and contemporary drama, the action is internal – a change of perception, a change of heart, or a new illumination or acceptance in a principal character. Sometimes action, even of this internalized sort, is entirely absent. *Note the key actions and turning points in the plot*:

- Who causes the main events to occur?
- Who actually acts?
- Is there one character who is the motor of the plot?
- Do several characters over several time periods, affect the action?

Remember that in some plays, the most dramatic action has occurred before the play begins.

With the skeleton of the plot events mapped out this way (use the worksheets in Appendix D), you can begin to understand how external action or plot can be the outward sign of internal action. This internal or psychological action is what Method actors call "the spine" of the play. In his study *The Human Image in Dramatic Literature*, literary critic Francis Fergusson re-examined the structure of this kind of action, which Aristotle said must have a beginning-middle-and-end. Fergusson wrote that when the beginning-middle-and-end of a plot are looked at as internal (as opposed to external) action, the pattern moves from a character's **Purpose** (beginning) to his **Passion** (middle) to his **Perception** (end). Most tragedies and comedies can be broken down into such a pattern of action.

In comedy the passion part of the action is very often a series of mix-ups and mistaken identities, or the kind of love test that will lead eventually to an affirmation of affection and often, on to marriage or a similar happy resolution. Sometimes, the perception leads onward to the hero's death (in tragedy) or to the expulsion or mockery of a blocking force or villain (in comedy). Often, the perception is a classic "recognition" scene in which one character comes to terms with himself, or with another.

Many postmodern plays, including the epic theater initiated by Bertold Brecht, do not follow such a strict, linear model. You'll usually find, however, that the action heads somewhere. Perhaps it's only to a final inevitable sense of futility, as in the plays of Beckett, or to a conclusive sense that something must be done, as in Tony Kushner's *Angels in America, Part I*.

Plots can generally be divided into three kinds:

1. **The climactic plot**: This traditional form of plotting begins with exposition of the problem or purpose, then builds through a series of confrontations or crises to a climax that moves forward towards resolution. Actions follow one another in a cause and effect pattern. Oedipus wants to know why a plague has visited Thebes? Finding the answer leads to finding out who he is. Very often these plays have a major plot and a minor plot, or several, called subplots.

2. **The episodic plot**: This form consists of a series of events that may take place over a long period of time in many different locales. Events may be related thematically to each other, instead of by cause-and-effect or in a single dramatic action. Brecht's *Good Person of Setzuan*, and Kushner's *Angels in America*, has an episodic plot. Shakespeare's history plays such as *Henry V,* are episodic, moving through many adventures and battles to demonstrate, in Henry's case, his fitness as a ruler.

3. **The cyclic plot**: These staged stories may have little action and may end where they began because their writers feel that such a structure best reflects human experience. However, even with a cyclic plot, there is often a sense of one cycle ending and another beginning.

Most plots are propelled by a purpose or desire in one or more of the characters, no matter how that motivation works itself out.

Here are a few examples of characters' purpose:

- In Shakespeare's *Henry V,* the title character has just become king of England and needs to establish his authority by freeing himself from his own youthful reputation for irresponsibility and also from the taint of stealing the crown, which was both his father's legacy and downfall. The wastrel Prince Hal, who frolicked through Eastcheap taverns with Falstaff, has to demonstrate that he really is kingly as Henry V. He must show his people that he has all the attributes – personal, political, moral, and even sexual – of a national leader.

- In Hamlet, the hero is instructed by the ghost of his father to revenge his most foul murder. The action of the play charts Hamlet's vacillation as he decides whether to carry out that command by testing and playing with those closest to him at the court – his mother Gertrude, who has disappointed him to the point of disgust by marrying his father's brother Claudius; his girlfriend Ophelia and her father Polonius; his close friend Horatio, and his not so close friends Rosencrantz and Guildenstern.

- In Cat on a Hot Tin Roof, Maggie the Cat wants to have a baby and carry on the Pollitt family line, thus impressing the patriarch, Big Daddy. Maggie's wish collides with her husband's frigidity and latent homosexuality.

- In *Topdog/Underdog*, a younger brother wants to become a master of the street game three-card monte and thus ascend to top dog, but the brother who taught him the game ends up blocking his way.

Think about your play this way as you read it, and determine whether it does have a three-part linear action – external, or internal, or both – or whether it follows a different plot trajectory as it moves towards its ending.

Character:

Characters are the people in a play. Aristotle viewed character as the moral force in theater. The actions of each character set off a chain of events, each linked by cause-and-effect, which constitute the plot. Classical and early modern drama, especially tragedy, tended to center upon one or two principal characters. But many other plays share the action, or inaction, among several main characters. Chekhov's plays tend to move this way, as ensemble pieces with as many as six characters (as in *The Sea Gull*) creating the interconnected society in which Chekhov plays his themes. Eight actors from the Tectonic Theatre Project took on multiple roles in *The Laramie Project* when Moises Kaufman directed it because he was trying to create a portrait of an entire town, not just to explore a single or even a few characters.

While you are reading a play for your assignment, think about how each character is depicted.

- Does he or she have any depth or complexity?
- Do the main characters change or at least reach a "recognition" or a "resolution?"

12

- If there is a main character or protagonist, is there also an antagonist who has an opposing desire or point of view?
- Are some characters "stock," that is, easily recognizable types such as the dreamy young lover, the macho, bragging soldier, the overworked mother, or the grumpy old man?
- Are the characters interesting and compelling? Do you find them credible? Likable? True to life and to your ideas about human nature?

Knowing what kinds of characters the author has created and sensing how they relate to one another and influence each other's behavior and the outcome of the play will help you know what to look for in those relationships on film.

This knowledge will allow you to assess the sensitivity of the casting in the film and the quality of the actors' performances.

Theme:

Theme describes the ideas and issues raised in a play. Most serious drama, including the lightest of comedy, engages audiences in ideas and issues as well as in characters and action. Themes are the meanings that can be distilled from reading a play. In the best traditional drama, theme is actually embodied in character and action. For example, having an outsider mentality, a sense of living in an alien world afflicts many of the tormented souls in Tennessee Williams' plays. When they clash with more thick-skinned characters, that conflict between the socially "normal" and the sensitive outsider becomes a theme, something larger than the play that contains it.

- One theme in *Henry V* is kingship – how it is defined, how it relates to politics and war, and more importantly, how it affects friendship and loyalty. The new King Henry V rejects his old friend Falstaff; critics and directors still differ about what that rejection says of Henry's character. Later, he approves the hanging of one of Falstaff's thieving cronies and debates with a common soldier about the monarch's responsibility for the souls of those fighting for him.

- Modern and contemporary playwrights including Ibsen, Shaw and Brecht stage discussion scenes in which characters directly argue various points of view about issues such as women's rights, or the justifications for war. In these situations, it's important never to confuse a single character's ideas with the author's point of view. Especially in discussion dramas, the nature of a character, his or her motivations, and your feeling for the character's honesty, intelligence and sensitivity will all affect your judgments about his or her points of view and the play's themes.

Questions about theme:

- Does the play seem to preach rather than embody its ideas?

- Is there a character that seems to be the author's mouthpiece, or one that you would consider the moral center or compass of the play?

- Do the characters that promote certain ideas seem likable? Do they listen to others and to opposing points of view?

- Does the action later undercut a character's statements or ideas?

At this point in your preparation, you might want to jot down a few revealing quotes that crystallize the play's themes. Such quotations may prove useful when you are writing your essay and looking specific details to illustrate your points. A strong quote, characteristic of the author's writing and revelatory of character or tone or theme, can provide an excellent starting point for such a review or essay.

Setting:

Playwrights are generally quite specific about the settings of their plays, especially if they are naturalists who believe that environment is a key to character or realists who wish to create the illusion of real-world people in everyday settings. Writers such as Beckett are also very specific about their non-realistic settings – the bare tree for *Waiting for Godot*, the earth that nearly buries Winnie in *Happy Days*. Other writers, however, including Shakespeare, are less strict about where the play should be set, and how the stage should be "dressed." When there is little such information given, the writer is clearly assuming either that the director will create a visual environment for the play or that his language will conjure a sense of place in the audience's mind.

Try to envision the play you are reading onstage, while remembering that other very important aspects of the design and atmosphere are costuming and lighting. What a character wears can be an extremely economical way of signaling who he or she is and where he or she stands in relationship to others. Like the set design, costumes can define period and place. Characters can then be spot lit to underscore their speeches, while transitions between scenes can be as simple as a blackout or as cinematic as a fade or dissolve. Follow the playwright's stage directions and note if there are any cues for lighting, music or other sound effects, such as the loud whack of the axes felling trees at the end of *The Cherry Orchard.*

Style and language:

These two characteristics are usually related. Prose, for instance, is the language of realism. Yet prose itself can have a lyrical quality as it does in plays by Thornton Wilder and Tennessee Williams or a jazzy swing as it does in contemporary plays by Suzan-Lori Parks or an argumentative complexity as it does in the works of the early 20th century author George Bernard Shaw. While reading, try to define the artistic style of the play, while realizing that some plays are mixtures in both language and style. Here are some of the major period styles in art and drama. You might want to look them up in the anthology's glossary, or search for examples of each style in an art history book.

- Classicism
- Renaissance
- Neo-Classicism
- Romanticism
- Realism, Naturalism
- Expressionism

- Absurdism, Surrealism
- Postmodernism

Contemporary directors will sometimes stage a play in a style different from the one in which it was written; they might even choose a style that clashes with the original. Director Peter Brook's famous 1970 production of *A Midsummer Night's Dream* went against tradition by using big blocks of symbolic color rather than literal trees or palace courtyards in the set. Keep this possibility in mind as you move towards watching the film version of your play.

Another aspect of style involves the degree of theatricality in the play script. Note whether the author calls for conventions such as music, mime, masks, heavy makeup, elaborate costuming, or such spectacular effects as storms or the appearance of gods from above or, as more recently we've seen, angels or hallucinations.

Tone:

Tone is perhaps the most subtle aspect of a dramatic world, and the one most easily misunderstood by both readers and directors. It is also the most challenging aspect of any theatrical work to put into words. The tone of a play – its quality of feeling, the precise nature of its comedy, the sincerity of its viewpoint, its lightness or heaviness of mood – is often difficult to ascertain on a first reading. Stage directors can choose to brighten, to shade or to darken the tone and atmosphere of a play in many ways – by the disposition of characters on stage, the physical reactions of characters to one another, the quality of the lighting, the volume, the speed, and the rhythm of the actors' speech, and by the use of music and sound.

Some guidelines to help you identify the tone of the play:

- See if the author has given any hints of skepticism or irony in the way he or she juxtaposes characters or scenes.

- Listen for speeches in which characters get carried away emotionally and determine whether the passion is justified, feels believably lyrical or rhapsodic, or seems unbalanced by reason or thought.

- Look for overreactions in characters, for a lack of reaction, for surprises and double takes, and for the hidden meanings in dialogue which actors call subtext.

- Be alert to both excesses and understatements in the language and what they might mean.

- Listen for silences and pauses. Read passages aloud to sense how they "play."

Step 2: Watching the film and taking notes

Once you have familiarized yourself with the play and also thought about the basic differences between stage and screen, as well as the different expectations you should bring to the two media, you are ready to watch the film. Assuming that you have the luxury of seeing the film either at home or in an academic audio-visual lab, you'll be able to stop and re-start the film to examine specifics. If that option is not available, you must be very alert as you watch for clues to the director's strategies.

In movies, you may find yourself noticing the setting, whether an interior, a cityscape, or a landscape, much sooner and more frequently than in a stage play. You may also find yourself drawn much more quickly into a kind of dream-like identification with the characters. As noted in the chart on page five, these are two major differences (and strengths) of filmic representation from theatrical. And so, you may sense that language has taken on a secondary role. You may become aware that dialogue from the play is missing. You may also begin to sense that various kinds of visual imagery have taken its place.

Textual cuts and other script changes:

Many filmed plays are just that, faithful documentations of the performed play with virtually no changes to the play script. The Gate Theatre-sponsored DVDs of Beckett's plays have this kind of fidelity to the language of the scripts, although they nonetheless use filmic devices. Kenneth Branagh's famously "uncut" *Hamlet* (1996) is very close to that description in its treatment of the script, and so is the television production of *Death of a Salesman* featuring Dustin Hoffman.

Look for meaningful changes by asking:

- Has the dialogue been cut or rearranged, or perhaps turned into a voiceover (as Laurence Olivier, and later Branagh did with some of Henry V's monologues and prayers)?

- Have certain characters been dropped from the film? Or combined with other minor characters or relegated to an off-stage role?

  - Has certain language been changed, "cleaned up" for a PG rating, for instance, or simplified because it was perhaps too dense in the play?

  - In "Cat on a Hot Tin Roof," the veiled homosexuality of Maggie's husband Brick, and the gay relationship of the two men referred to as "sisters" who previously lived in the house are important elements of plot, character and theme. But in the 1958 film starring Elizabeth Taylor, Paul Newman and Burl Ives, the most explicit references to homosexuality were dropped or made oblique. The film was produced when a stringent Motion Picture Code was in effect. The Code banned such references, censoring the language of Hollywood features. So in this case, you might note whether these changes affected the film's exploration of the "mendacities" tearing the family apart.

  - Does the director reverse the order of scenes?

- Are certain speeches and plot elements left out to simplify?

- Is the language of whole scenes cut because the camera has recorded real imagery as it pans across a natural scene or a room on location? Photorealism may have replaced verbal description or implication. The playwright's descriptions are no longer necessary? Or are they?

As you make note of the changes, deletions, or more subtle differences between script and screenplay, remember that you'll eventually be looking at these for clues about the director's intentions, not for evidence to find him or her guilty of being unfaithful to the playwright.

Casting and acting:

Perhaps the most obvious element of the film treatment of a play is the director's choice of actors to assume the characters' roles. Because film and video use close-ups made possible by the camera, these media tend to create popular "stars" and celebrities out of actors far more than the stage does. If the film you are studying has just one, two or three principal roles, they may be cast with the familiar faces known as "stars." If so, how do these actors handle the emotional and technical demands of their roles?

Taylor, Newman, and Ives, for instance, starred in the 1958 film of *Cat on a Hot Tin Roof*, and although the film proved emotionally effective with audiences and a career-boost for all of the actors, some students of Tennessee Williams prefer the 1985 Showtime television movie directed by Jack Hofsiss with Tommy Lee Jones as Brick, Jessica Lange as Maggie and Rip Torn as Big Daddy. Not only are the cuts restored and the themes made more explicit, but also Lange takes a more fiery and humorous approach to Maggie. Jones, who is no matinee idol like Newman, suggests both physical and emotional pain in Brick. Noting the emotional quality and credibility of the acting is especially important in such basically realistic dramas. Other elements of the acting crucial to the film's effect include the casting of subordinate roles (Big Mama, for instance) and the vividness of scenes in which the main players are not the focus. In other words, is there a strong sense of ensemble creating a unified atmosphere and effect, or is the film dominated by a star ?

The latter question is especially pertinent to a film such as *Hamlet.* You will easily find examples with Laurence Olivier, Kenneth Branagh, Mel Gibson and Ethan Hawke in this coveted leading role. If you watch such a film dominated by character, take special note of the soliloquies as examples of the actor's skill in conveying the main character's thoughts and emotions. These scenes will also help you to characterize the ways in which the directors have chosen to film these crucial solos, thus revealing their insights into the hero at various points in the action. As you take notes on the actor's and the director's approaches to these scenes, be ready to note other things:

- Does the public Hamlet – the man who dispatches Rosencrantz and Guildenstern, gives instructions to the players and frightens Ophelia with his madness – seem to be the same man who reveals his near-despair in the soliloquies?
- Explore the depiction of his other relationships – to his mother, his treatment of Polonius, his friendship with Horatio, and his mood in the graveyard scene. Billy Crystal plays the gravedigger in the Branagh Hamlet film. What does he bring to this scene of blackly humorous comic relief?

By noting such aspects of any lead actor's interpretation you may begin to form an overall assessment of the performance and of the film.

When writing about more limited release films such as the Gate Theatre's DVDs of Beckett's plays, you are likely to see many actors unfamiliar to you, and a few that have appeared in movies and television shows. In this case you might ask yourself whether the director has melded the various actors into a company – a true acting ensemble in which every member seems to be serving the play and the director's vision of it.

Finally, you need to be certain you understand the difference between two very different acting styles:

- a presentational approach is when the actor speaks directly to the audience and both he and the viewer are aware that this is a play, not the illusion of everyday reality.

- a representational approach is when the actor creates the illusion that the "fourth wall" has been cut away and we are overhearing and seeing real life.

Although most films require representational acting, those that are inspired by Brecht, and some docudramas, such as those by Anna Deavere Smith, take a more presentational approach. Also, the newer movie musicals often veer back and forth between the two styles.

Later, when writing your review or essay, you may only need to identify two or three of the actors playing the leading roles. Even so, it helps now to form an overall estimate of the quality of the director's casting.

- Does the director have an "eye" for matching actor to role?
- Are the smaller supporting roles, especially if they are stock or archetypal characters, better cast – and more memorable than the principal actors?
- What effect does this have upon your response to the film and your assessment of it?

Camera work:

The chart (p. 6) contrasting film and theater noted that in a theater space the audience is free to look at whatever part of the stage appeals to the eye, whereas in film, the director (i.e. holding the camera lens) can manipulate the viewer's attention by drawing the eye to whatever the camera is focused upon. This effect is most true of the close-up, when the camera records the reactions of a face, which may belong to the character speaking or acting but sometimes focuses upon the face of a person listening or reacting or being acted upon. Subtleties of facial expression project to audiences in a live presentation only if the theater is small. But on film, the viewer's identification with the characters is created by these intimate close-ups.

Think about how the use of the close-up affects the presentation of your particular play.

- Has some language been deleted in favor of facial expressions or gesture?
- Do characters we know only from afar in the play become more significant in close-up?
- Does the director shift attention away from the main, obvious characters or toward more minor figures? What is the effect?

Long shots allow the camera to take in a large swath of action, landscape, crowd scenes or good-bye scenes from a distance. Along with the medium shot, these different distances of camera and actor are among the film director's most basic tools of story telling. Many films end with a long tracking shot as the camera recedes from the final action or confrontation, pulling viewers away with it and back into the real world.

Experienced feature film directors set up a variety of shots, creating a rhythm and interest just in the movement from one kind of shot and distance to another. Still, fine films such as LaBute's *In the Company of Men* have been made with a very still camera, and very few changes of location. Note where your film fits into this spectrum of possibilities.

Setting and opening up:

Films are seldom shot on a stage set within a theater. There are, of course, interesting and important exceptions to this rule – those 1950s live television broadcasts, for instance, were shot continuously in real time on the equivalent of a very large stage in a television studio. The early and closing scenes of Laurence Olivier's *Henry V* were shot on a replica of London's Old Globe Theatre where the play premiered four-hundred years before. Later, this brilliant and unusual film "opens up" to the battlefield and castle shots at the center of the film. The Beckett DVDs were shot in television studios and originally aired on Irish TV.

More frequently, however, filmed plays move the action into realistic environments, taking advantage of the camera's ability to move about, capture people and action from many angles, and substitute images captured by the camera for stage sets built in imitation of real places. Kenneth Branagh's film of *Much Ado About Nothing* was filmed in Tuscany and moves about the Italian countryside. Both time and place are transposed from Shakespeare's script, and this "opening up" includes vigorous outdoor scenes with the men returning home from war on thundering horses.

Note the setting of your play on film and ask yourself the following questions

- Is the setting different from, an enhancement of, or the same as the setting you noted when you read the script?
- What effect does the new setting have upon your response to theme?
- If the new setting seems jarring, could it be intentionally so, or was it simply a bad choice on the part of the director?

Lighting, costuming, music, and mood:

As with a play production, costuming and lighting are key visual components of a film and can greatly enhance – or diminish – its effect. Again, the best costume reveals character and the distinctions among characters almost at a glance. It can suggest such aspects as social class, attitude towards self and sexuality, level of education and taste.

Lighting can be more sophisticated in film than onstage. It can take on an artistic dimension that involves such elements as contrasts between light and shadow, variations in intensity, bold or subtle use of color, and emotionally satisfying or exciting use of cuts, fades, cross-cuts and dissolves. (See Glossary for the meaning of such terms.) Note whether and how the use of light affects our response to the film. Orson Welles was a master at creating atmosphere through lighting, shadows and silhouettes. He often achieved painterly effects like Rembrandt's by shining light on his actors from below, deforming their faces. The entire genre known as film noir is built on a suspense created in large part by evocative and mysterious shafts of light in an otherwise dark and moody setting. Not surprisingly, the lighting designer for a film is supervised by the cinematographer or director of photography, for the camera can only record a scene if, how it is illuminated.

If lighting is often the element that makes a film feel coherent visually, music can be the element that makes it cohere aurally. This is why many film producers commission original scores from composers. Many of these take on a life of their own. They carry within the musical metaphors, the conflicts and the resolutions of the play. Alex North's score for *A Streetcar Named Desire* proved so durable that it became the basis for a ballet on the play's themes. The bittersweet piano music of Chopin is often in film adaptations of Chekhov. Other scores include a theme song conjuring *Star Wars* or *Jurassic Park* with just a few bits of melody.

Note whether the music in your film seems to underscore the emotions, conflicts, crises and resolutions of the plot. Or does the music overdramatize these events? If the music distracts from the characters and plot or overwhelms them, perhaps it is ill chosen. If, on the other hand, you find the music appropriate, describing it may help you define that elusive element of tone.

Editing and visual rhythm:

As you watch the film try to become aware of how it is put together, that is, how it segues from person to person, action to action, scene to scene. Usually movies strive for what critics call "fluidity" or "cinematic" flow and we are not aware at all of the editing process. In actuality, directors create a film shot-by-shot, and it is up to the director and editor to then assemble the results of those shots into a whole that might be highly dramatic in its contrasts, or smoothly lyrical or even jangly and upsetting.

This editing process creates a rhythm for the film, something like a musical rhythm. Certain films unfold slowly, for instance, and you are aware of the camera lingering over a scene or allowing the characters long silences, pauses or moments of contemplation or internal emotion. At the opposite extreme are those films that seem to jump when they cut from scene to another short scene. The 2003 film of the musical *Chicago* uses this technique in the vaudeville scenes, creating a nervous, excitable rhythm suitable for the material. Become aware of the rhythm of your film.

- Does it seem to follow the rhythms of the play as you read it?
- Does the film use cinematic resources to create a different kind of rhythm?

- Does the film use these resources to change the pacing and rhythm for different characters or different sections of the action?

Like tone, rhythm is difficult to write about. Finding a vocabulary for writing about these qualities, however, will greatly enhance the precision of your review or essay, and in the end, will reward you with deeper knowledge of how theater and cinematic art are created.

Step 3: Rethinking the play and the film

Now that you've made yourself aware of key elements in the play at hand and in the film based upon it, take some time to review your notes and rethink your observations.

You might ask yourself these questions:

- Did the film visualize the play as you imagined it or very differently? What might account for the differences?
- Did the film seem stagy or artificial, or did it feel natural and engaging?
- Did the film seem to be about the same issues, ideas, and emotions as the play or did it change for you thematically on the screen?
- Were you aware either of the focus (i.e. the camera) staying still, in one place, or at the other extreme, were you aware of it moving around too much?
- Did the film create a coherent world in which you were engrossed? Or did a single aspect of the film – an actor's

interpretation, the music, the setting, costuming, editing – seem to take over the film and disrupt its world and your involvement in it?

As you answer these questions for yourself, you will begin to form your critical opinion about the film's effectiveness and artistic quality. But before you write your essay, you will need to refer to your notes, as well as your impressions, your feelings and your tentative judgments in order to think about the film director's strategies. Section II of this guide will walk you through that process, the **analysis.** Sometimes first impressions can be misleading or limited. The analysis section will help you test those observations and impressions so you will be fully prepared to write your review or essay.

II. ANALYZING

Now that you have explored the fundamentals of the play and film, it's time to attempt to discover more about the director's approach. Each film is necessarily an interpretation of the original play, with the playwright's language and themes filtered through the mind and imagination of the film director and his team of collaborators. Because each director brings his own background, education, prejudices, artistic taste – and even the morning headlines – to the script, the film will yield clues to his interpretation and to his strategies for communicating it. After examining that interpretation and those strategies, you can determine whether the film is artistically coherent, emotionally compelling, and effective on its own terms. Few topics generate such heated opinions, often hotly contested, as the degree to which plays (and other literary works) are "realized", "translated," "adapted," "distorted" or even "ruined" when they are interpreted by filmmakers.

Step 1: Deciphering the director's strategy

In general, there are three basic approaches or modes of filming a play. As with all such categories, however, these are not meant to be reductive, nor do they exhaust all the possible approaches. Some films employ several approaches, moving from the realistic to the expressionistic (or filmic) depending upon the scene. Nonetheless these three basic kinds, first outlined by critic Jack Jorgens, should help you begin to analyze any play-on-film in terms of the director's strategy.

Modes:

- **The Theatrical Mode**: Film becomes a medium for transcribing a stage production It has the look and feel of a performance created for a theatrical space and played before a live audience. Each shot (or take) tends to be long and continuous. The camera tends to be quite still. The acting is filmed in such a way that each scene seems framed by a kind of theater proscenium arch within which the viewers' eye sees the actors speaking and gesturing. These are without the expansive movement that would be permitted by an outdoor location, or the "opening up" of the script to realistic exteriors and interiors. Most of the British Broadcasting Corporation (BBC) videos of Shakespeare's plays were created this way, as transcriptions of stage performances. Two video productions of Sam Shepard's "True West" – one for PBS with John Malkovich and Gary Sinese, another for Showtime with Bruce Willis – take this approach. We see the actors on the same set upon which the action would take place in a theater.

The strength of this kind of movie is that the script can stay pretty much the same as in the stage play, without a lot of cutting or rearranging. The acting can have the same continuous and verbally articulate quality it does in a theater. The disadvantages are that the movie or video can feel static, even dull, because there is less movement of both actors and camera, and long speeches on film or television can sometimes be difficult to follow.

- **The Realistic Mode:** Most mainstream American films are created in this mode which takes advantage of the camera's ability to photograph things of all kinds – vast landscapes, the nooks and

  crannies of homes, details of expression on a person's face, armies marching, cars racing, lovers kissing. Few of these kinds of scenes can be represented directly onstage, and so the realistic mode begins to present the film director with possibilities. He can augment a play script with action scenes, use a shot panning across a landscape to replace a description of it, or use a close-up of a person thinking with a voice-over of that person's thoughts (onstage, this would be a soliloquy).

The obvious strengths of this mode of filming are its familiarity with the world we live in and its potential for variety. The settings may be spectacular or minimalist, beautiful or harsh, almost documentary in their starkness. Realism, however, can also provide too much detail, the kind of emphasis upon visual richness that overwhelms language and the actors. External fidelity to "reality" does not necessarily support deeper, more internal truths and emotions. Especially with eloquently written dramas, the realistic mode can flatten the poetic language, making the words seem precious or too arty in a visual context that looks like everyday life. Directors of realistic films sometimes cut out other artful devices that give the play its special character. Without symbolic props or emblematic groupings of characters or poetic flights of fancy, certain literary and formal qualities of the play can be lost, and the play can be warped beyond recognition.

- **The Filmic Mode:** This mode allows the director to play with the techniques of filmmaking itself, thus translating the play from a mostly verbal to a more completely visual medium. The director might emphasize the artifice of the film, carefully designing the composition of each shot as if it were a painting, or making us aware of the lighting, or cutting from scene to scene so quickly and abruptly that we are always aware this is a film, not the illusion of reality. Such an approach often involves using anti-realist techniques, and emphasizing the non-literal. Here, the director attempts to reflect an inner world, one in which imagination, memory, and emotion are the key elements, rather than plot, realistic setting, and conflicts among characters. The plays of Samuel Beckett lend themselves particularly to this approach, for characters often speak in non-sequiturs and the stage directions call for strange symbolic objects that are strikingly visual —Winnie's burial mound in *Happy Days* or the gnarled tree in *Waiting for Godot.* Similarly, the last plays of Shakespeare, and some of his tragedies, are filled with spectacular storms, epic journeys, ghostly apparitions, and miraculous events that lend themselves to the filmic approach.

The strength of such an approach is in its freedom to move from image to image unconstrained by time, space and the usual laws of cause-and-effect. A dream-like or a purely pictorial logic can organize the pattern of images. Music very often plays an important role, creating atmosphere and tension. That freedom, however, can also be a liability if the filmmaker indulges in dazzling technical tricks for their own sake and with little concern for the actors, the story telling, or the script's themes and meanings.

In addition to choosing the mode of filming, the director chooses how closely he is going to adhere to the original play – not just in terms of its language and dialogue but also in its style, setting, and the various tensions and balances between scenes and characters. If you have already noted whether (and how) the director and screenwriter have cut, rearranged and edited the play script, or even replaced its language, you are already on your way toward determining which kind of treatment the director is using. The following list of possibilities is not exhaustive, but it should begin to get you thinking about the nature of the director's fidelity to the script.

Kinds of film treatments of plays:

- **Presentation:** This term describes the treatment that feels closest to the playwright's original intentions and emphases. The director (and screenplay writer) alters the original play script as little as possible and does not choose to highlight a single interpretation or to focus on particular elements of the script. Thus the audience is free to explain and experience the work on its own. Such an approach, while evenhanded, can be dull and monotonous, as much a reading as a performance.

- **Interpretation:** This term refers to a treatment that involves shaping or emphasizing certain elements of a play so that it conveys the director's point of view of it. When a director cuts speeches in order to emphasize (or de-emphasize) a certain aspect of a character, or when he updates the setting of a play to make it more relevant or universal, then he is interpreting the work. In addition to thinking about how the screenplay differs from the play script, you might return to the question, did the film seem to be about the same issues, ideas and emotions as the play or did it change for you thematically on the screen?

- **Adaptation:** This term refers to the kind of treatment in which the director and his collaborators use the play as a springboard for their own parallel work of art, in much the same way that a novel is "adapted" into a movie. The film becomes a kind of variation on the themes of the play, sometimes very different from the intentions of the original. Baz Luhrmann's *Romeo+Juliet* is a good example of a film adapted from Shakespeare's play for a different age and audience, though it does maintain Shakespeare's language. Situations, themes, and characters remain similar even though the screenplay, settings, costuming and other particulars may be very different.

- **Recontextualization:** This term refers to the kind of film treatment that changes the setting or context of the play. Many, but not all adaptations, do recontextualize the play as well; many, but not all recontextualizations go beyond the change in setting into the realm of adaptation. Often, these films update the story for contemporary audiences, making them more easily relevant. But recontextualizing a play for the movies can also frame the story in ways that make us see the themes and the play itself differently, in the same way that the *Back to the Future* films mock the popular culture of the 1950s, for instance.

Some examples of recontextualizing:

- Chekhov's *Uncle Vanya*, usually set in late 19th century provincial Russia, has been explored in a fine film adaptation by Wallace Shawn and Andre Gregory called *Vanya on 42nd Street*. It's set in the 1990s in an old New York warehouse where an acting company is rehearsing the play.

- Actor Kenneth Branagh set his *Hamlet* film in 19th century Prussia instead of 12th century Denmark. Presumably this actor/director wished to underscore the militarist aspect of Shakespeare's tragedy that is so often overlooked in favor of Hamlet's psychology.
- Luhrmann's *Romeo+Juliet* places Shakespeare's 14th century Italian love story in a late 20th century Southern California beach town where gangs are fighting with guns with the brand name Sword.

Setting

The setting is a design element that can take on much greater importance in film than in the theater. You will have noticed by now whether the director set the film in the same time and place as the original play (like the 2002 commercial film of Oscar Wilde's *The Importance of Being Earnest* with Colin Firth and Reese Witherspoon) or moved it either forward or back in time. Perhaps the filmmaker left the time and place vague, a kind of "universal timeless" as in Julie Taymor's Shakespeare film *Titus*. If the director made such a change, what is its effect, and why do you think he made the change? By setting her film in such an eclectic, timeless environment, Taymor not only moves Shakespeare's script from ancient Rome, but also generalizes its themes.

Often directors want to make the themes of their films universal, so they try not to pin down the time and place too specifically. Or by moving the time forward a bit, and moving the action away from England or the United States to some more "exotic" locale, they might shake up the viewer's accustomed response to the play, and again point to the universality of the themes and emotions. Director Richard Longcraine moved the time and place of his 1996 film of Shakespeare's *Richard III by* setting it in a fascist European dictatorship of the 1930s. That time period parallels the original, late medieval setting of the play in that both periods generated leaders who were murderous tyrants.

Thinking about why a director chooses a particular time and setting, then looking at how the designers realize that concept can be a key to unlocking the interpretation and strategy of any play on film. Remember, however, that merely shifting the time and place does not guarantee a better or more relevant film. You must evaluate the meaning and appropriateness of the shift.

Step 2: Comparing visual to verbal

Your analysis can now move on to the ways in which the director has used (or not used) the greater visual freedom of film to realize his interpretation. Be sure that you have determined which mode or combination of modes the director has employed and also which treatment or combination of treatments (presentation, interpretation, adaptation, recontextualization) best describes the film. Then you can begin asking the appropriate questions about how the work holds together as a film.

- If the film is basically in the **theatrical mode**, and seems also a straightforward **presentation** of the play, does the director employ any of the special strengths of the film medium at all? If not, does the film seem dull or monotonous? What is it in the film that grips your attention? An actor's interpretation perhaps? If so, does the director or cinematographer use close-ups to deepen character and emotion?

- If the film seems to carry a specific **interpretation** or concept, review which scenes and speeches, if any, are cut. Speculate about why. Do these changes point to the director's specific view of character or theme? Or is language simply dropped and replaced by visual images captured by the camera?

- If the film is in the **realistic mode**, does the wealth of physical detail, including costuming help to illuminate the story, or does the film bog down in too much unrelated imagery, or action, or spectacle?

- If the film is an **adaptation** and especially if it is in the **filmic mode**, does the director create a world with similar emotions, tensions, themes and intensity as the original play, even though it may look different? Does the film feel like a valid response to the play or does it seem to distort the play's meaning or express a wrong-headed interpretation or concept? Why?

Now that you have noted the director's approach, and some of the cinematic conventions and devices the director has employed, you should be ready to start writing about the film. In the third section, we will offer suggestions for organizing your thoughts and your notes and for shaping two kinds of assignments – the short review, and the longer thematic essay. These are by no means the only kinds of assignments you may be asked to write, but applying theses suggestions judiciously, and in tandem with the glossary of film terms and critical terms in Appendix A, should help you further hone your critical skills so you can write confidently about your play on film or video.

III. WRITING: DESCRIPTION, ASSESSMENT, AND JUDGMENT

Now you are ready to write your review or essay. As always, you should begin by creating an outline that groups together the elements of your discussion into sections, each with the notes, observations, and details from the film that will illustrate your points. Depending upon the type of paper you are called upon to write, and the length required, you will first have to determine how complex your thesis can be and the level of detail you will be able to present to support it. But whatever the assignment, your own critical writing should do the following:

- **Describe** the relevant portions of the film so the reader can "see" what you saw; this means using clear, vivid language with as much specific detail as possible.

- **Assess** the director's interpretation, strategies and intentions; this means using words that place the work in its category and context and convey its values.

- **Judge** the effectiveness of the film (or the scene, or the actor) and the degree of its success or failure in realizing the director's intentions.

Step 1: Getting the facts right and your notes in order:

To begin, review your notes to be certain you have gathered the relevant facts about the film and its creators. You should have answered the following basic questions about the play and the film.

Finding the credits:

Because the credits for some films roll by so quickly, you may have trouble locating the names of the designer or cinematographer when you watch a film in class, or in the college or university media center. A thorough and accurate Internet source for films and videos is Internet Movie Database. Search for IMDB.com, type in the name of the play/film, and you will be presented with a list of all film versions of the play and their dates. Be sure to click on the correct director and date for your film or video, and you will be linked to a list of credits for the movie. These also link to mini-biographies and further credits for each of these contributing artists and craftspeople.

1. The play:

- What is the full title of the play and who is the author?
- When and where was it written?
- What is the time and setting of the action? Your anthology is the best source for this information.

2. The film director:

- Who is the director and what is the date of the film?
- Has the director presented a logical, coherent interpretation of the play? What mode has the director adopted for the film: theatrical, realistic, filmic or some combination of these three? Does this approach seem appropriate to the story and the director's interpretation of it?

- Are the actors well chosen? Has the director created a feeling of ensemble in the cast?

3. The actors:

- Who are the principal actors and what are the roles they play?
- Who are the most important secondary actors and what roles do they play?
- Who are the strongest performers in the film? The weakest? How do these performances affect the film overall? Attempt to be precise in describing noteworthy performances; avoid abstract and well-worn adjectives such as "memorable" or "interesting" and instead try to describe exactly how the actor works, and what he or she does, or how he or she speaks – all the qualities that make the character communicate to you.

4. The designers:

Lighting:

- Were there any particularly striking lighting effects? Was there an overall pattern to the evocative use of light?
- Try to describe any artistic dimension created by lighting such as contrasts between light and shadow, variations in intensity, use of black and white or sepia tones, bold use of color, and emotionally satisfying or exciting use of cuts, fades, cross-cuts and dissolves.

- If this element strongly creates atmosphere, you should learn the name of the lighting designer and mention him or her in your essay.

Settings:

- Were there any particularly striking scenic designs or landscapes – either outdoor locations or interiors that establish time, place, and mood?
- Was there a coherent sense of visual design at work?
- Can the emotional effect of the designs be described or were they find them overwhelming? If yes, then you may want to learn the name of the film's designer to give proper credit or criticism

Costumes:

- Is the costuming appropriate for each character, and the time, place and style of the settings?
- Are the costumes an eclectic selection for the period? How?
- Often the same artist designs sets and costumes; if these are particularly striking and effective, name the designer and describe what specifically makes the costumes contribute so strongly to the film.

Music:

- Is the music an original score or a pastiche of classical, rock, or pop tunes?
- Does the music help to create the tone and atmosphere of the film? If so, describe the kind and quality of the music.

- Is the music too overpowering and distracting?
- Is it a substitute for creating atmosphere visually?

5. The cinematography and editing:

- Do the camera angles and movements help tell the story, convey the theme, and maintain your attention or do they call attention to themselves in ways that are unrelated to the director's intention?
- Does the editing – the movement from shot to shot – create a rhythm that supports the storytelling style and themes?
- If either of these two elements seem particularly strong, or particularly weak and distracting, you might name the artist responsible and describe their contribution specifically, so you can briefly assess credit or blame.

Step 2: Crafting the thesis and writing the paper

Many kinds of writing assignments may be required as you learn more about drama, theater and plays on film and video. Depending upon the emphasis of your course, you may be asked to write a short review of a film, to compare and contrast two film treatments of the same play, or to analyze two or more actors in the same scene – for instance, Olivier, Branagh and Mel Gibson in *Hamlet*; or Dustin Hoffman and Lee J. Cobb in *Death of a Salesman*; or John Malkovich and Bruce Willis as the volatile Lee in *True West*. You may also be asked to write a longer critical essay discussing a single theme in the play by comparing the ways in which the playwright and the film director develop that theme.

You may be asked to write a research paper that involves historical and cultural material, such as sources and inspirations for the play and film, or the possible motives for a director's recontextualizing the play on film.

In this section, we offer suggestions for organizing your thoughts and your notes, and for shaping two kinds of assignments – the short review, and the longer thematic essay. These are by no means the only kinds of assignments you may be asked to write. But applied judiciously, in tandem with reference material in the glossary of film terms, and critical terms in Appendix A, these suggestions should help you hone your critical skills so you can write with confidence about your play on film or video.

The review:

Typically, the review is a relatively short (2-3 pp) response to the film written soon after you, the critic, have seen it. This type of criticism doesn't usually require footnotes or quotation from sources other than the screenplay and perhaps another critic or two. The following four-part structure will help you organize your review and present your thoughts coherently.

- **Introduction or "lead":**

  The best reviews begin with a sentence that gets the reader's attention, a vivid statement that strongly conveys an aspect of the film and suggests the author's opinion of the work. Sometimes a quotation, with a description of how the actor spoke the words, makes a good introduction;

sometimes a word picture of a representative scene or technique will serve to pique the reader's interest. A good introduction not only conveys information, but also suggests the tone, energy, emotional quality, and theme of the film. Many professional critics create two-paragraph introductions to their reviews.

The first paragraph serves as a scene-setter to draw the reader in, while the second provides the more factual information (name of film, director, principal actors, date, and author of play upon which it is based) that a reader wants, and needs, to understand the work. Reviews seldom state their argument in the form of a thesis. But, by this point in the review, the reader should be able to sense the critic's overview of the film, a view that will come into sharper focus as the writing proceeds.

- **Summary of the play and the film director's approach:**
  This summary is an especially important element of your review, it familiarizes a reader, who may not know the play or film, with the central elements of plot, character and theme, and with the film director's approach to these elements. However, nothing is duller than a mere chronological summary of plot events. You must choose the **significant** elements of plot and theme, the central issues the play engages, and the **most representative** directorial strategies for realizing them.

When the playwright and the film director seem to be taking different approaches to the storytelling, this is the place to briefly summarize those differences.However, there are often thimes when plot, theme, and character conflict are nearly inseparable as in such plays as *"Death of a Salesman, Hedda Gabler, Hamlet,* and *True West.* In these cases, the lead actor's performance may be the key to understanding the film's treatment of the play. If so, a description of the actor's interpretation of character would be called for. Such descriptions should be precise, calling up images of how the character speaks, reacts, feels and moves.

- **Analysis of the directorial approach, the design choices, the acting, and their contributions to the whole:**

    In this section, usually several paragraphs long, you will need to dissect the various contributions to the strength and/or weaknesses of the film. Since the director bears the ultimate artistic responsibility for all elements of the film, his interpretation or concept of the play should be described, whether you agree or disagree with it. Provide enough detail so that the reader can see your perception in the film. If you disagree with the director's interpretation or approach, you should feel confident enough to say so and offer your own interpretation of the play. Then show how the film director has gone wrong. Your analysis will benefit greatly from specific evidence such as lines from the text, descriptions of particular scenes that illustrate the director's approach, and the contributions of his collaborators.

An analytic example:

Here's a section from critic Anthony Lane's comments about Luhrmann's *Romeo +Juliet* film as they appeared in a 1996 issue of *The New Yorker* magazine. Note how specific and energetic the writing is, its tone echoing the qualities of the film.

> Luhrmann is thirty-three, but Shakespeare was even younger when he wrote *Romeo and Juliet* and both play and film have a just-you-look-at-this quality, easily read as young men's riffs. The one dab of brilliance in Luhrmann's picture is his notion that Romeo (Leonardo DiCaprio) does not speak his monologues on the topic of Juliet's perfection but jots them down in a journal. He is a poet – your basic horny teenager trying to collect and prettify his thoughts on paper – or if you prefer, a Shakespeare in the bud. This tallies beautifully with our apprehension of the play's youthfulness, of a poet still wrestling his unnerving dexterity into dramatic submission.Lane makes very clear, to readers who may not have seen the film, the young and vigorous qualities of Luhrmann's adaptation for the screen.

Very often, when the performance of the principal actor is the hinge upon which the film moves, you will need to analyze the nature of that performance, providing specific details, both physical and emotional. The following is an example of wonderfully specific writing about Vivien Leigh, the actress who played Blanche DuBois in the original Broadway production of Tennessee Williams' *A Streetcar Named Desire* and the film version of the same play.

Another good example:

Pauline Kael, the most influential film critic of the second half of the 20th century, wrote this description of Leigh's performance in her *5001 Nights at the Movies*:

> Vivien Leigh gives one of those rare performances that can truly be said to evoke pity and terror. As Blanche DuBois, she looks and acts like a destroyed Dresden shepherdess. No one since the early Lillian Gish and the almost unknown, plaintive Nadia Sibirskaya of *Menlimontant (1926)* has had this quality of hopeless feminine frailty. Shakespeare must have had a woman like this in mind when he conceived Ophelia.

That Dresden china doll conjures very different, but just as precise, images as those in Kael's description of Elizabeth Taylor as Maggie in Williams' *Cat on a Hot Tin Roof*. Taylor "looks very desirable, and the cast is full of actors whooping it up with Southern accents," she wrote with ironic and slightly grudging respect.

If an actor is miscast, describe what's wrong with his or her performance. If there is no sense of cohesiveness or ensemble in the acting, describe a scene that is limited or ruined by this flaw. On the other hand, if the actors, the lighting, the costume, the set designs, the music, and the camera work all seem to be contributing to a unified effect, you might mention representative examples of each of those elements, in a single scene, to illustrate the film's artistic unity. If one or another of these elements is jarring or overwhelming, this is the place to mention it.

- **Concluding judgment about the effectiveness of the film and its relationship to the play that inspired it:**

Your conclusion should summarize and reiterate the points you have been developing, and state a final judgment about the film's quality. It is important that your evaluation be fair and even-handed. Very often critics write mixed reviews, which balance the strengths and weaknesses of a film. Very few works are unmixed successes, meriting the kind of thumbs-up or thumbs-down response given by TV reviewers. Do not be afraid of writing a negative review if the work deserves it, or a very positive one for that matter. Though such unadulterated "raves" or "pans" are the exception in serious critical writing, your judicious analysis of the film and lively appreciation of its parts, should still make for an intelligent and readable review. Pauline Kael summed up her review of *A Streetcar Named Desire* by placing her negative criticisms in balance with the much greater strengths of the film:

> "Elia Kazan's direction is often stagy, the sets and the arrangement of actors are frequently too transparently 'worked out,' but who cares when you're looking at two of the greatest performances every put on film and listening to some of the finest dialogue ever written by an American?"

Kael and other well-known critics have been reviewing films all their lives. As a beginner, don't expect to write as well or as knowledgeably. Still, by following the guidelines outlined here, you will be able to get started and produce a coherent, lively and analytic review.

However, certain easy tricks or gimmicks for opening a review should be avoided. Here's how one student mistakenly attempted to get his reader's interest. *A poor example:*

> I left the house a bit late and in my hurried frenzy to complete this assignment found myself driving in the wrong direction, away from the movie theater. To my horror, as I approached the Pacific Beach exit, I realized my error. After a few quick turns I was back on the freeway, speeding and weaving my way to the Edwards Cinema, where a trailer for the next Disney film was still playing as I rushed into my seat to see a most enjoyable film adaptation of *The Importance of Being Earnest*, a comedy by Oscar Wilde that I had seen once before in high school.

This writer's personal troubles have nothing to do with his analysis of the film and probably don't belong in the review at all – certainly not in such a prominent place.

Here's how another student more effectively introduced his review of the same film with Colin Firth, Rupert Everett, and Judi Dench.

A better example:

> Oscar Wilde's witticisms once again catch the audience's attention in the hilariously absurd film adaptation of *The Importance of Being Earnest*, directed by Oliver Parker. Wilde subtitled his play, "A Trivial Comedy for Serious People." It seems that Parker has decided that "serious" people no longer exist and so he's created a trivial comedy for movie-lovers who might never set foot inside a theater to see the play. While Parker cuts and rearranges dialogue, sends the two central couples chasing all over London, and adds a bill-collector following one of the men, he also retains most of the famous one-liners from Wilde's script in the film.

This student has not only introduced his topic, but has also tipped the reader off in just one paragraph that this will be a mixed review.

The longer essay:

Typically, this kind of essay is at least five pages long and develops a clearly stated thesis about the film or video. You can include longer quotations from the play or screenplay, from the artists involved, and from other critics whose opinions support or differ from your own. Such an essay will probably require citations and/or footnotes. You should discuss with your professor the format required. Whatever the format, the effectiveness of your essay will be determined by the clarity of your thesis and the specificity of the illustrations and examples that support it.

Most writers find it useful to group their notes in patterns. By examining the answers to your questions about theme, approach, directorial strategy and the artistic realization of it, you may see a thesis emerge naturally. Perhaps you will discover that the film version has so cut up the text and been constrained by the camera so that the play script is no longer recognizable or compelling. Critic Sylvie Drake thought so of the Showtime presentation of George Bernard Shaw's *Heartbreak House.* (Academy films released the video in 1987.) Drake's essay provides something of a model for an introduction.

> *Heartbreak House* is Shaw's darkest, most difficult and most prophetic play, full of tenderness and foreboding, wit and apocalyptic vision and, for all of those reasons, it is the Shavian play that most frequently misfires. But in 1983, New York's Circle in the Square presented a burnished revival of it – so subtle and resplendent, with Rex Harrison at last playing his age and delivering such an unforgettable Captain Shotover – that it could easily be termed definitive.
>
> PBS' Great Performances series has produced an abridged version of it – again with Harrison, the winsome Rosemary Harris as eccentric Hesione, Dana Ivey as prim Lady Utterwood and Amy Irving superb again as plucky and coolheaded Ellie Dunn.
>
> So why has the edge been dulled?
> (*Los Angeles Times,* January 24, 1986)

Note how it moves from a general appreciation of the play and a significant staging of it, to the question that her commentary will answer. Such a question could readily lead to a thesis for a longer paper on the effects of too much cutting on the play's themes (here for the sake of a television time slot) and on the effects of too claustrophobic an approach to filming.

As you have no doubt learned in many English classes, a basic structure for such an essay will include at least these parts:

- Introduction to the topic and statement of thesis
- Related idea and observation, with very specific examples
- Supporting idea with specific illustrations
- Another supporting idea with specific details
- A conclusion that reiterates your thesis with a sense of inevitability

One favored approach to learning about drama and performance, whether on stage or screen, is to compare two actors in the same role. Such a project reveals not only individual acting talent and specific styles, but can also highlight different directors' approaches, and indeed, different facets of the same script. The compare-and-contrast structure for an essay is time-honored and relatively easy to use as a template for organizing your notes. Actors, individual scenes, even entire films, lend themselves to this approach, depending upon how long your paper can be.

Caryn James, the television critic for the *New York Times* concluded her review of the Showtime presentation of Sam Shepard's *True West*, starring Bruce Willis, with this mixed response:

This unbalanced production won't rival the definitive "True West," which played Off-Broadway twenty years ago with John Malkovich and Gary Sinise (who directed it), or even the Broadway version two years ago (2000) with Philip Seymour Hoffman and John C. Reilly alternating roles. But Mr. Shepard's play remains deep, enduring and outrageously funny with its many layers about family and identity. This latest "True West" is worth watching for Mr. Shepard's words and Mr. Willis's performance and for the hint it offers of how exhilarating it might be to see Mr. Willis onstage next to actors who can keep up with him.

(*New York Times*, August 12, 2002, E, page 1)

James had outlined some of the ways in which Willis' performance as the wild desert rat Lee overshadowed that of the less experienced actors in his theater company. She also noted that because of this imbalance, the director seemed to play up the comedy in the play nearly as much as its menace. If you were to write on *True West*, you might consider watching both the Malkovich and Willis videos, either to compare-and-contrast the two performances for your assignment, or simply to enrich your knowledge of the play by seeing two interpretations before you write about an aspect of one. This is one of the great benefits of plays on film and video: they are available for multiple viewings.

Research papers about plays on film can yield exciting and revealing results as well. Here is a bit of biographical history about the first sound film of a Shakespeare play, Columbia Pictures' *The Taming of the Shrew*, starring Douglas Fairbanks and "America's

Sweetheart," Mary Pickford. The writer is Barbara Hodgdon in her "Katherina Bound; or, Play(K)ating the Strictures of Everyday Life."

> (The film) is perhaps even more infamous for its credit line, "by William Shakespeare with additional dialogue by Samuel Taylor," the director. A contemporary cartoon shows a bust of Shakespeare at the Library of Congress being replaced by one of Taylor.....According to Pickford's autobiography (and to her sympathetic biographers), Fairbanks tamed the 'shrew' in real life as well as dominated her before the cameras: he not only played jokes, delayed shooting schedules, and failed to learn his lines, wildly increasing production costs, but relegated his co-starring wife (and co-producer and co-financer) to a lower place in the production hierarchy. Writes Pickford, "The making of that film was my finish. My confidence was completely shattered and I was never again at ease before the camera or microphone." (from *Shakespeare on Film*, ed. Robert Shaughnessy, New York, 1998)

Hogdon's essay proceeds with a complex analysis of how Pickford's image as Kate in the film exploited her reputation as a grown woman pretending to be a little girl, while also showing her as a kind of tomboy who "cracks a mean whip." The much-filmed *Shrew* offers another possibility for compare-and-contrast papers, because it has been often filmed, usually by such popular stars as Fairbanks and Pickford.

Whatever your subject, however, we hope that the forgoing suggestions for preparing, analyzing, and writing your paper will help you organize your thoughts, sharpen your critical skills, and deepen your appreciation of plays on film and video. The worksheets in Appendix D will help guide your note-taking. Other appendices to this guide include a glossary of film terms and critical terms, as well as a quick refresher course in vivid writing and a checklist for your paper. Use these appendicies and glossaries. Good luck.

Appendix A

Checklist for Self-Editing Your Writing

1. Does the opening paragraph introduce not only the work to be discussed but also your attitude toward it?

2. Does the opening paragraph engage the reader?

3. Do you have the facts straight and all names spelled correctly – the play, author, date, director, actors, designers, etc.?

4. Have you chosen a suitable design or structure for your review or essay – and then held to it?

5. Have you described and analyzed the key elements that distinguish the film from the play or other film adaptations of it?

6. Have you described the director's interpretation of the play and his or her strategy for filming it?

7. Have you assessed the contributions of the relevant designers?

8. Have you assessed the quality of the acting overall, and of individual actors?

9. Have you supported your judgments about the directorial interpretation or concept, the design elements and the acting with specific illustrations and examples from the film?

10. Have you concluded your review or essay with a strong statement that sums up and reiterates your assessment of the film?

11. Have you cited all quotations accurately?

12. Have you formatted the paper properly with consistent margins,   type size and spacing?

A Refresher Course in Effective Writing

Effective writing is clear, direct, vivid and precise. As you prepare, write, and edit your review or longer essay you might keep in mind a set of simple, time-tested guidelines. Several of these were formulated by writing teacher William Strunk for his classes, which included the essayist and children's book author, E.B. White. White published his teacher's wisdom in a handy reference called *The Elements of Style*. Here are some of Strunk and White's rules and a few of our own, with examples:

- **Omit needless words:** not, Algy came off to me as a loner and standoffish; but, Algy appeared aloof.
- **Use the active voice:** not, the set was designed by Catherine Martin; but, Catherine Martin designed the set.
- **Provide vivid detail:** not, Brando's memorable performance; but, Brando's intense, edgy performance.
- **Use figurative language:** not, Dench's Lady Bracknell looked prudish and tough; but, Dench's Lady Bracknell combines the poise of an aristocratic prude with the blocking power of a Pittsburgh Steelers' tight end.
- **Keep related words together**: not, Branagh flashed a grin riding into the sunset; but, riding into the sunset, Branagh grinned.
- **Use parallel construction:** not, Hamlet's mother Gertrude, uncle, Claudius, and Ophelia who is his girlfriend; but Hamlet's mother, Gertrude, uncle, Claudius and girlfriend, Ophelia.
- **Use strong verbs:** not, the girls sit down and act like they don't care but actually are really angry; but, the girls suppress their seething rage.
- **Avoid clichés:** not, "like the plague." but "like an allergen.

Glossary of Terms: Film and Criticism

Cut – An editing term that describes a transition between two or more scenes or shots, without traditional optical transitions. Film is merely spliced together, so the frame appears to move quickly.

- **Cross-cut** – The technique of editing together two actions or sequences that are spatially (or even temporally) separate from one another. This technique is primarily used for showing parallel actions between two subjects, such as in a chase scene, or a phone conversation.
- **Jump-cut** – A type of edit that breaks the fluidity of a subject's motion on the screen. This technique does not follow what is known by cinema theorists as the "thirty degree angle rule," a tradition that requires the camera to be placed 30 degrees apart from its previous position when filming and editing a subject. Following this rule shows the audience that camera placement and changes of angle are deliberate. Otherwise the image will appear to "jump" on the screen. Formally, a jump-cut is considered a cinematic *faux pas*, unless it is done for purely stylistic purposes.

Diegetic Sound – Derived from the term "diegesis" or the narrative world of the film. This type of ambient sound can be easily identified as part of the scene.

Director – The artistic force behind the "look" of the film. The director is in charge of the transformation of the written screenplay into a visual narrative. Ideally, the director should have the most say in all artistic choices from casting, to design and editing.

Dissolve – An optical effect that gradually merges one series of images with another by briefly superimposing the two series .

Fade – An optical effect that changes the light output on the screen. A "fade-in" refers to a dark screen gradually getting lighter until a picture can be clearly seen. A "fade-out" refers to the picture on the screen gradually becoming darker, until the audience sees black. The term "fade" can also refer to sound gradually growing louder or softer respectively.

Genre film – A term referring to the grouping of films in categories by their similar stylistic or thematic traits, e.g. the Western or film noir.

Mise-en-Scene – The arrangement of, and relationship between all of the elements of film in a single shot or frame. In French, literally translated, "the placing of a scene."

Montage – A style of filmmaking that combines images and/or sounds into a coherent narrative. In the United States, montage is traditionally used to show the passing of time. Filmmakers in the Soviet Union pioneered montage as a stylistic movement in the 1920s. In France, montage refers simply to editing.

Narrative – The story creating the momentum of a film. Narratives can be traditionally expressed through dialogue. Visual images can also produce a cinematic narrative such as those in a montage.

Producer – The financial backer of a film, whether a person, group, or corporation. It is the producer who gives the "green light" to a project. The producer selects a director suitable for the project, and monitors the progress of the shooting and production.

Location – A place in which filming occurs. Location shooting refers to a place outside the studio that has been approved for filming. Malls, schools, or city streets could be considered filming "on location."

Screenplay – A film's action, dialogue, camera movements, and effects in a written sequence – usually also visualized on a storyboard – to be shot to produce the final product.

Set – A constructed background, or scene in a film. Normally, most sets are constructed within a production studio.

Shot – The basic unit of film involving both the position and distance of a subject from the camera.

Close-up Shot – A camera angle that frames a subject very closely, as in a full view of a subject's face.

Framing – What appears on the screen.

Medium shot – A camera angle that frames the subject from the waist up.

Long shot – A camera angle that is taken at a great distance, usually with a wide-angle lens. The long-shot can be used as an establishing shot, which situates (or establishes) the subject's relative position in the scene.

Tracking shot – A term that describes the motion of a camera. A tracking shot follows (or tracks) the subject(s) with a camera seated on a smooth track, often pulling away from the action or characters at the end of a film.

Voice-over – Typically in the form of narration or internal monologue, a voice-over refers to sound that is "extra-diegetic" which means that it does not come from the narrative world of the scene, but is rather "supplied."

Worksheets

. Understanding the Elements of the Play:

PLOT: Note the key actions and turning points in the plot.
- Who causes the main events to occur?

- Who actually acts? Who is influenced by the action?

- Is there one character who is the motor of the plot?

- What is the central conflict?

- Or do several characters over several time periods affect the action?

CHARACTER: Note the names, qualities and functions of the main character's
- Who is the main character or are there several principals? Name them.

- Does he/she/they have any depth and complexity?

- If there is a main character or protagonist, is there also an antagonist who has an opposing desire or point of view?

- Are his/her/their conflicts external or mostly internal? Describe the conflicts.

- Do the main characters change or, at least, reach a "recognition" or "resolution?"

- Is the main conflict resolved at the end or left ambiguous?

THEME: *Note the development of the theme.*
- Is the play about something more than the characters' conflicts, actions, and concerns? At what point did you become aware that the action or dialogue was "about" something larger?

- What scenes contribute to your understanding of the play's themes?

- State the play's main theme as succinctly as possible without oversimplifying.

I. Understanding the Elements of the Film:

The director:

- Who is the director and what is the date of the film?

- Has the director presented a logical, coherent interpretation of the play? State an overall judgment to be detailed in the Analysis section.

- Describe specific scenes that are especially effective, and/or scenes in which the director fails to pull all the elements together in a satisfying way.
  1. Scene 1—

  2. Scene 2—

  3. Scene 3—

- Did the director cast the film well? Has the director created a feeling of ensemble in the cast?

Screenplay:

- Note any major textual cuts and other script changes. How do you account for the important changes? What effect do these changes have upon your assessment of the film's themes?

- Note any characters dropped from the film version. Do these omissions change your feeling about the main characters? About the themes? The richness of the work?

Acting:

- Is the style of the acting **presentational**? In other words, do the actors sometimes speak directly to the audience, making the viewer aware that this is a film, not the illusion of everyday reality?

- Or more likely, do the actors take a **representational** approach to create the illusion that we are overhearing, and seeing, real life?

- Note the **names of the actors** in major roles and the role they play:
  ACTOR   CHARACTER

- Evaluate the **actors' performances**, especially the three leading actors.
  1. Are their speaking voices clear, accented, or colorful?

2. Are their physical presences strong, strange, or appropriate to their characters?

3. Is their energy charismatic, off-putting, or lethargic?

- Does the **acting** convey a shared sense of purpose? Do the actors seem to play off one another or is there one star?

Setting:
- Note the **setting**. Describe it and whether it has been "opened up" beyond what is possible onstage, or changed from what the play suggests. Is the new setting effective in framing or enhancing the play's action, characters, and themes?

- Did you notice any particularly striking scenic designs or landscapes – either outdoor locations or interiors that establish time, place, and mood?

- Did there seem to be a coherent sense of visual design at work?

- Can you describe the emotional effect of the designs?

Other design elements:

- Costuming
    1. Is the costuming appropriate to each character? Does it reveal character or call too much attention to itself?

    2. Are the costumes eclectic or ambiguous about period? Why?

    3. Often the same artist designs sets and costumes; if these are particularly striking and effective, describe specifically what it is that makes the costumes contribute so strongly to the film.

- Music
    1. Is the music an original composition or a pastiche of classical, rock, or pop tunes?

    2. Does the music underscore emotion in the film or help to enhance atmosphere? Is it overwhelming? Describe the kind and quality of the music.

- Lighting
    1. Does the lighting help to create mood, atmosphere, and drama?

2. Describe the overall look of the lighting – such as the use of bold contrasts, of shadows, or an unobtrusive approach to name three extremes. Provide at least two examples of scenes in which lighting is an obviously important, even critical factor in communicating meaning or emotion.

Cinematography and editing:

- Are you aware of the **camera work**? Are there many close-ups? Are they effective? (The Glossary of film terms will help you distinguish various kinds of shots.)

- Do the **camera angles** and the movement of the camera help to tell the story, convey the theme, and maintain your attention, or do they call attention to themselves in ways that feel unrelated to the director's intention?

- Does **the editing** – the movement from shot to shot – create a rhythm that supports the storytelling style and themes?

- If either of these two elements seem particularly strong, or particularly weak and distracting, **name the artists** responsible and describe their contribution specifically. This may be the director if, as in the case of Orson Welles, he is an **auteur**.

III. Evaluating the Film:

Director's choices– mode and strategy:

- What **mode** has the director adopted for the film: theatrical, realistic, filmic, or some combination of these three?

- Does this approach seem **appropriate** to the story and the director's interpretation? If the director's strategy cuts against the usual reading of the script, is there a logic to this different approach?

- Is the **storyline** clear and comprehensible? Or is clarity not a goal?

Director's choices– theme and interpretation:

- Does the director use **landscape, or props, or costuming, symbolically** in order to convey certain themes? Do any of these devices keep reappearing, like a **recurring theme** in music?

- Does the author/director/viewer's attitude towards the themes or ideas change as the film unfolds? Try to clearly state whether the the elements outlined contribute to a **coherent interpretation.**